Book of Exodus

To Deanna —
I hope you enjoy the book!

BOOK OF EXODUS

poems by
Kathryn Smith

Kathryn Smith

 Scablands Books   *Spokane, WA*

Published by Scablands Books
scablandsbooks.org

ISBN-13: 978-0-9907525-6-1
ISBN-10: 0-9907525-6-9

Managing Editor: Sharma Shields
Editor: Maya Jewell Zeller
Cover art and book design: Keely Honeywell

Printed in Spokane, WA by Gray Dog Press

CONTENTS

Four

Five

"Everything
That may abide the fire was made to go through the fire..."
—Galway Kinnell

"The family's principal entertainment, the Russian journalist
Vasily Peskov noted, 'was for everyone to recount their dreams.'"
—*Smithsonian*

One

Psalm/Flight
(with Psalm 121)

I lift mine eyes to
the hills. From whence cometh
my help? My help comes from
the Lord, who
made heaven
and earth.

Gaze upon
what we are running from
The Lord
will provide a sign and
turn wilderness
to loneliness

He will not
cause
your foot to stumble,
and he that watches over you
will not slumber. Indeed,
he who watches over Israel
will neither
slumber nor sleep.
The Lord watcheth
over you; the Lord
is the shade at your right hand.

Transformation

has no wings

has only this running

Our running
is fearful but it is not
running away

The sun
shall not smite thee
by day, nor
the moon by night.
The Lord keepeth you from
all evil; he guardeth
over your soul. The Lord
will watch
over your going out
and your coming in
now and

We run toward
believing
in the emptiness of
its freedom
The heart's frantic wall, pulsing with
the breath,
does not want release
it wants
to beat
to beat
to beat you

for evermore

What Akulina Carried

the frame, the beam, the batten

treadle   heddle   harness   shaft

the reed (which resembles a comb, but this is for fiber, for thread, is necessary)

what weights the warp to keep it taut
weighs our journey
(jettisoned for stones)

what can be unwound to free of constraints
to free (me) (the self) (to free)

shuttle   shuttle

over time it takes
its own shape
as pieces break
as shuttles wear to splinters
frame reframed sawn timbers to crags

(but if hair is like thread and can be unsnarled and is taut is tight is difficult
to break, then why not the hair, the hair held woven, the reed for both the hair and the thread
the hair both hair and thread the hair to clothe the body entire)

Exodus

We keep count:
forty days or
forty years.

We will not
be tempted.

The beasts are blessing, for they
were with Christ, the snake
an intercessory Aaron,

the tongue whose hiss
God answers.

Even if the river
were made of milk, we
would not
drink it. We cross
mouths closed

  touch it   and it
crashes down
it drowns
what lies
behind me

        *(get
        behind me)*

Then I set
the bush
alight

Through the Eye of the Needle

The World is
decoration. As for embellishment,
soot-smudge will do.
My sleeves
have survived fire. We have yet
to be consumed.

The Gray Forever

At times, the night is disguised
and animal: A bird. A wolf. A bird
with talons. Sometimes, a snake
losing skin. I would like to abandon
certain layers, to shed each winter
delicate scales. Like snow.
Like leaves elsewhere or in another
season. Sometimes the night
is autumn itself, dim but never
dark. A gray wanting.
And willing to go either way.

Of Wine

What Jesus drank he taught us
to avoid. In this land, no milk,
occasional honey. If you
can endure the sting.

Diary

Callus.
Hunger.
52 days until season's last frost.
Too few days until frost again.

We mark time until we celebrate
The Day The Lord Freed Us.

We live with what
the Lord has provided in this vast
and abundant loneliness.

We are not pilgrims. We
are already here.

Two

The Children Learn the Alphabet

a: alpha: beginning
a: adam: the first
b baptize b briar beware
what sounds the c, some calico christo
       call calvary cry of the crow
what sometimes sounds *suh*: celestial *suh* ceremony
      suh sister (no, stupid)
      cerebral (what is that) *suh* city (what is that) *suh* cipher (no) cedar (now, now)

O cedars of Lebanon, cedar house, cedar tree, O God of the tent-living wanderers
cedar the tree the bark we must fashion the wood it is said never rots

d devil (of course) Dmitry (of course), d drowning disciple d doubt
e exile, e exodus (though why not x, crossed out crossing over)
for egg then (what is egg) for echo then, echo:
      the sound of your voice crossing over itself the sound of one voice repeated

Lullaby

savior's little bearchild
nevermind of milk

savior's little serpent
sleek as coiled silk

set the flame before you
set the bush alight

slither through the burning bush
close your beast-eyes tight

Where No Crumb Can Save You

In the stories, children wander the woods alone,
falling to the trap of sin. There are ways
to survive. You cannot let the witch
lure you with her house of sweets.
You cannot fear the wolf. I am the girl who

plies the forest with darkness as her ally.
I dig the traps with my own hands, bare. I
am ready to wrestle the lion, just as the Book
prepared me. To emerge unscathed after I've
shared its bed.

Hide and Seek

Sister, can you see me? Can you see me
now? Do I yet blend
with the mud of my surroundings?
I cover myself with something that crusts.
Flower me a garland, a necklace
of nothing. No flowers in the scrub so we have
to make do. Scrub of the forest floor, scrub
against the skin. What I long for, what I intend
to reach. This mud-bath ornament lets me be
alone. Leaves for eyes, whatever crosses my path, I see
but it cannot see me.

The Children Learn the Alphabet

field fallow furrow frog
famine flaxen Father God
fire fog-filled freedom

g *guh* gutter (stutter)
gander gallow garden green green gathering green

fallow
gallow
hallow
I

Bread from Heaven

Shake the trees
to bring the manna down.

Spread the cones.
Wait while the sun's heat dries them.

Beat the cones
to coax the manna out.

Sift seeds from spurs
until fingers tingle,
sticky with pine sap, numb
from the work. Cup
a hand to hold
a cone's worth of pine nuts, touch

a tongue to the palm and
taste and see God's goodness, how

He feeds and feeds until the mouth
knows only this bitter
persistence.

Work Song

What's that in your kettle,
Fannie Fettle, Fannie Fae?
What's that in your kettle?
Will it last another day?

What's that in your basket,
Little Liza, Little Lou?
What's there, I'm so hungry,
Nearly anything will do!

Catch the fish, little brother,
And we'll feed it to our mother,
Catch the snake, little other
For our mother has the flu.

Pick the thorns from the berries,
Gather rowanberry leaf,
Shuck the husk from the pine nuts,
they're the only cure for grief.

Mother says, *Don't be wasteful:*
suck the bone when there's no meat.
Father says we must be faithful
if we want something to eat.

Starvation Couture

I have torn this life out at the seams
and reshaped it. Our clothes
hang like sacks
on a line from our shoulders.
Bone pegs. Wind-
billowed. No cords to cinch our shrinking
waists. This is wilderness fashion.
Sister, don't give me
that pouty expression: so last
year. So gaunt and wanting. Shoes
are so completely out. I mean,
so out we cut away the soles and
boiled and ate the leather.

Skin of No Consequence

To be cast to the wilderness is to be
with the beasts. The beasts do what
I ask. The beasts do what I please.
Has anyone seen you? Have you yet
been named and counted?
Please form a line according
to size, then to number
and ferocity of teeth.
A thing without a name
is not a thing. Sorry, creature.
The count is over. I have
no numbers left, which makes you
unthing. Sinew for another purpose.
Fur and meat on bone.

The Children Learn the Alphabet

sin sister salvation starvation the snake
        the snake the
thee   thine thou

u as in you
the sound the u makes is you   is un-
        unworthy umbilical ugly
(the ugly words all start with u)

(with)

(you)

zephaniah   zachariah   zero   zero

Three

What instruments do we need
but our voices? What music
but the telling of our dreams?

The Girl Who Has Never Seen a City Dreams a City

Papa laughed when I described it.
Not every one is the same, dear child. The buildings do not cut
the sky in one straight and perfect line. The roofs angle
like they are trying to explain, each house
an arrow that knows it can never
reach the heavens to which
it eternally
points.

She Dreams of Heaven's Bounty

I sat down with the Lord but could not see
his whole face. At the table, I was given
no portion. I saw only his mouth as the Lord
raised bread to his lips, then meat, his teeth
tearing flesh from the leg of an animal,
juices dripping from his fingers to the floor. I thought
the watching could feed me. I peeled fig after fig
with my eyes until the Lord said my name:
>   *Agafia,*
>   *crouch and eat.*
Beneath the table, his feet. His sandals.
And the sumptuous crumbs. The everlasting.

She Dreams Salvation

In the year of the great famine, I dreamed
one rye sprout survived the June frosts,
breaking through a crust of pea shoots,
limp and blackened with cold. It unfurled
skyward, a visible rising toward brilliant spring light.

Waking, I prayed my dream true. I built a fence
to keep the creatures out. It was still dark.
I could not see what I was protecting.

Her Sister Dreams of Luxury

A room to myself.
A pump to draw the water
directly indoors. A new dress
in bright colors, its collar
chafing. A goose-down mattress
brimming with quilts.
A mule to draw the plow.
Flowers and the taste
of sweetness. To be
scrubbed clean.
Shovel. Salt. Someone
to place his hand on the back
of my neck and lift
the weight of my hair.

She Dreams the Fall

There is one book in the world. I dream
its words into new arrangements.
Noah does not survive the flood. Eve
and the serpent curse Jesus' fig tree.
She is not man's rib, but the jawbone
of an ass, her hair the strength
of Samson. She dreams her own
Delilah, someone to seduce.
A dream within my dream.
I wake ashamed.

She Dreams Her Own Undoing

I had shoes. Shoes! The taut pull of laces
to keep me upright, soles a holy barrier
between body and earth.

My sister had none, so I shared them—one shoe
at a time. To give both would be to let comfort
seduce her. She would never give them back.

Both of us, then, feared the leather's ruin.
So the rabbits came, gnawing pea shoots to the root.
The harts nosed out the last heads of lettuce.
Cucumber dribbled from a cub's silky chin.

He stretched a paw toward me in vegetal
offering, but my feet were fixed:

one shod on the safety of firmer ground,
one bare and sinking at the edge of the plot.

She Dreams Revelation

As in the Book of Daniel, four beasts
rise from the churning sea. The kingdom

comes, and we must choose between two halves:
wings or horns, flight or fearful countenance.

In my dream, I ask for both, am given
one of each. Worthless. Off-kilter, stuttering the sky, I

can neither pierce the enemy nor rise above him,
neither devour nor swim when the four winds

stir up the sea. It's these dreams I stumble on
when I wake, hair knotted from the tossing,

knowing more now than the Book allows.

She Dreams of Motherhood

I dreamed a cat
pinning the wings
of a hawk. I dreamed
chickens, their eggs
like silk on the tongue,
mother told me,
though I have never felt
such cloth. And the cat—
to have something
to lap at milk, a small animal
to nest beside me despite
its fur and my
lack.

She Dreams a Common Language

I dream the yard full
of domesticated beasts:
hens and goats and kittens.
Dark comes and they all curl
in the bowl of me,
lapping at my breasts.
Could my body feed?
A hunter is no hunter without
his dog. They speak, despite
their lack of common language.
What rises from my body
does not satisfy. But when
I dream, we all
lie down together
on the new earth: the feline
with the avian, the lost
with the found, trapper
and trapped, to catch but not
to eat.

Four

Satellite

How long I have lived
with these trees, their promise
of companionship. How long this certain-
color sky. I enter the wild wood and it
absorbs me, its scent a seal against
my skin. I am here
to be swallowed.
To learn the nocturnal lessons
of creatures immune.
As the canopy thickens
above me, a whisper: *We will devour.*
We will envelop. Teach me,
great forest, the supplications
of the inanimate,
how to speak a hollow vow
absorbed by this mothering wood.
Show me the path to the clearing,
where I can marvel
at the new stars, bright
and deliberate. Their watchful turns
make quick work of me, calculating
every possible way
I would break.

Psalm II in a Windstorm

look, the mountains

    have fitted their arrow to the string,

        to shoot the dark   bird;

    what can the   rain do?

    for   If the heart is   destroyed,

    how can   I Flee   like a scorching wind

to heaven.

the LORD's eyes shall be the violence.

    the refuge

              is in the gaze .

    The LORD tests the bow, and the wicked bend,

     For the LORD loves

coals of fire, sulfur, and wicked   humankind

and

hates the   lover of his face.

Beast Body

I made my skin of leaves. Clean ones.
My sister, she skinned herself down
to the beast body, the wolf tree, the we
who can do no wrong in the eyes of our
Lord. We are cedar children crossing
a frozen river. We know how to survive.
It's easy as dreaming, easy as fear when
you face the beast you are.

Belongs to the Earth

The peels of potatoes spring beneath the feet.
Oh, the moldy cushion.
Oh, the rotting bed. I'm bled. For the body consists
of organs. For the body consists
of the fall. Stain and
flesh. We read
sinew. Read *dry bones*. For the body
consists of spirit   is filled by it   is overwhelmed.
For the body consists of rot.
For the world turns round by it.
For the ground beneath our feet is full
of potatoes, waiting to show their leaves, to signal
the tuberous growth. And what is not eaten
we lie upon. For we do not see,
yet we understand.

New Vision

The night of the full moon
we gorge ourselves on bilberries

and do not sleep. Bloated
with wakefulness, we hunt

the wolf. Its eyes cannot best
our eyes. Clumsy

fur-thing, never covering
its tracks. My brother

will strip it and wear its
skin against his skin, both coat

and disguise. I am here
for its teeth

to string from swamp grass
and hang from my neck.

The Council

Each eye is the eye
of beginning. When spring
uncoils the shoot, we can only
give thanks if we are still creatures
in need of food and not buried
beside the waiting potatoes,
feeding the soil from which they rise.

Rehearsal for the Apocalypse

As the world was ending, we decided we'd
better choose our steeds.
Copper for me, black for my sister.
Dmitry would take the pale horse,
exercising his flair for the dramatic.
Father said it was not in keeping with the
Good Book to play such a game, not with
Hell at the threshold, banging down the door.
I've never been able to picture it: Satan
just standing there, his fiery hand curled to a burning fist,
knocking without setting everything alight.
Last spring there was such a late frost we lost
most of the garden and mother
nearly starved. I've always believed the end would
open the door in a gale of frigid air and take us all at once.
Pale horse or no, this wilderness could
quench any fire, even that foretold
revelatory burning. Sister stands by her choice,
saying black is the color you want when the world
turns around. Saying copper is ugly, and only
unfaithful girls choose it: girls who look to
Venus when the reckoning comes, who choose
water over fire, who primp and preen like Esther for
Xerxes, who never call on the name
Yahweh until the end, when
Zeus' thunder rains down, and none can abide it.

Her Sister Plots Departure

When Father speaks of The Liberation
I hear her whisper *exile*. Her small cairns
line the Western Wood, the path
she stakes, leaves cached to hide her.
Each step she takes is a small
betrayal, unraveling a sacrifice.
They had so much to fear when they fled.
We who have always lived
in freedom have nothing to fear
but God alone.

Psalm 42 in a Windstorm

As with a sword in my bones,   I come
 in the night
my prayer   will say

      God I thirsteth
      I went from the land of Deep noise
      unto oppression unto
(mourning hope reproach praise continually my soul in me:)
      the deep and yet

Yet I shall remember
      the hill   the hart   the living   the house
(for God before God thy God thou in God unto God thy God in God why go I O God my God)
      the voice of joy   the multitude

for I had kept these things :
      enemies   lovingkindness   disquieted countenance of day time

      God I
panteth

      why art thou
      When will I
      Why art thou

My tears are gone

gone As waves my soul
      my forgotten health

      the multitude panteth
pour out thy waterspouts God

Why art Where is Why thou Where is and why art thou

when shall
the water brooks   appear

　　　　O soul disquieted　　　　soul

for rock hast been my meat
　　　　my soul is night,
and billows within me:

 O my God, remember my life

　　　　my soul a song :   help

She Hears the Voice in the Wilderness
(with Psalm 29)

The voice of the LORD breaks the cedar trees;
the LORD breaks the cedars of Lebanon;

the LORD makes Lebanon skip like a calf,
and Mount Hermon like a young wild ox,
Sirion like a young unicorn.

The voice of the LORD bursts forth in
lightning flashes, it divides the flames of fire.
The voice of the LORD shakes the wilderness;
the LORD shakes the wilderness of Kadesh.

The voice of the LORD makes
the hinds to calve
and makes the oak trees
writhe and strips the forests
bare.
And in the temple of the LORD all are crying,
"Glory!"

The voice destroys.
The voice is the trap that snares the sable.
The voice connives.
The LORD trips the feet
of young animals and burden beasts and animals
we only imagine.
The LORD speaks fairy tales.

The voice is thunder, could tell the thunder
to cease but does not; sets fire
to the trees; sets the earth
quaking.

The animals give birth at the sound
of the voice. The voice
causes our birthing and our bleeding
and the wind (the voice the LORD) uproots
the trees
and though few can abide it
we praise.

Five

Tracing the New Stars

Man has made them in his quest
to be like God, believing stars
should travel, the celestial
revolving earth. See how they blink out
each warning. See—
the new constellations shift,
confounding any future Abraham. Who
am I kidding: We subtract and never
multiply. There is no prophecy I
can think of we are equipped
to fulfill, unless you count dying
in the wilderness. Or if this
is the garden from which Adam and Eve
were banished, and we have been locked
inside, where the Tree stands
stripped of its fruit.

What Remains

One soot-black window, a kettle worn through
   Nothing new, nothing ever new

One broken loom, one holy book
   For what is holy is only is lone is lonely

Some strips of birch bark, woven taut
   What can this vessel hold without hands to first create it

Tatters which once resembled clothing
   Such a makeshift patchwork, such a stitched-together existence

A small cache of seeds, dry leaves for tinder
   It's hard to breathe sometimes, how close our bodies

Store of potatoes, dwindling
   And tools for digging

One grave
   And tools for digging

Discovery

When they came to us, they brought sugar and flour.
They brought T-shirts reading *Expo '74*.
They brought the word *T-shirt*, and the shape of it.
The drape of it. There was news of a war
that had come and gone. Salt
and soap. But if we are sanctified we are not
unclean. If I never looked back, I'm no pillar,
though we ache for its mineral bite.

They Show Him Television

Dream after dream
and the dreams
are not my own.

Alphabet of New/Alphabet of No More

apple	apart
beacon	brother
companion	brother
decide	disappear
dream	dream
flashlight	forbidden
flour	forever
friend	hollow
grief	hunger
illness	loneliness
need	mother
oat	only
possible	pure
salt	sanctification
sated	separate
satellite	sister
taste	star
television	threshold
tool	trap
visit	vision
voice (of others)	voice (see mother)
war	voice (see sister, brother)
world	wilderness
wilderness	world

They Teach Her a New Way of Counting

They ask my age, then apologize,
thinking I have no way to separate
one day or year from another.

We are no barbarians.

There was the Time of the Great Panic:
Savin thought he had lost the sun's angle
and we prayed continuously rather than miss
the appointed time of prayer. Then prayer
revealed to us the hour.

In the new keeping, we are further from
the year of our Lord, but surely closer
to his coming.

Diary

I cannot say if I hoped for this day
or feared it. To imagine so many
tastes on the tongue. What is necessary?
Mother is dead because she let me eat.
Now these Strangers say there is no need
to hunger. I do not even
dream of it anymore.

Dream Without End

And when I entered that dream, I stayed there,
in the realm of new civilization. Beasts roamed
the broken streets. My one desire
was to save the fledglings that fell from nests,
abandoned by their mothers. Even when

I woke, I stayed there, tending wounded animals
who trip on fractured paths. My instinct
is folly, and there is no way
out, for dreaming is its own
wilderness. Once I have crossed
the threshold, it disappears. The sky
brightens, then
closes me in.

Notes and Acknowledgments

In 1936, Karp and Akulina Lykov and their two children, Savin (age 9) and Natalia (2), fled their village to escape religious persecution, taking with them seeds and any possessions they could carry, including a Bible and a loom. They set up a homestead in the Russian taiga, where two more children, Dmitry and Agafia, were born in 1940 and 1943, respectively. The family lived in complete isolation until geologists doing survey work came upon their homestead in 1978. The poems in *Book of Exodus* are drawn from this family's story but are not an attempt at biography and are largely fictional. I am indebted to an article in *Smithsonian* magazine ("For 40 years, this Russian family was cut off from all human contact, unaware of World War II," by Mike Dash, published at smithsonianmag.com on Jan. 28, 2013), and to the book *Lost in the Taiga: One Russian Family's Fifty-year Struggle for Survival and Religious Freedom in the Siberian Wilderness* by Vasily Mihaylovich Peskov, published in 1994.

The poems "Psalm/Flight (with Psalm 121)," "Psalm 11 in a Windstorm," "Psalm 42 in a Windstorm," and "She Hears a Voice in the Wilderness (with Psalm 29)" use text from the King James Version of the Bible, sometimes with modifications.

I am grateful to the following publications for giving first homes to some of the poems in this book: *Duende*; *Lilac City Fairy Tales Vol. 1*; and *Rock & Sling*, which featured several poems as a chapbook titled *Tracing the New Stars*.

I am deeply grateful to those who helped make this book possible: Scablands editor Sharma Shields, for believing in this book from day one and never looking back; Maya Jewell Zeller, who helped shape this manuscript from its early days and saw what it could be even before I did; Keely Honeywell, for so deftly capturing my vision for this collection in her beautiful cover design; Laurie Lamon, Christopher Howell, and Nance Van Winckel, who taught me to hone and trust my own voice; the community of poets who surround, encourage, support, and challenge me, and whose friendship I would be lost without, especially Thom Caraway, Linda Cooper, Jeffrey Dodd, Ginger Grey, Amy Munson, Laura Read, Laura Stott, Emily Van Kley, Ellen Welcker, and Maya Jewell Zeller (and to Ellen for telling me about "pine mouth"); the artist residency and 2013 winter community at Holden Village, where these poems first came into being; my parents, for encouraging my unsustainable ambitions; and Jake, for everything.

About the Author

Kathryn Smith's poems have been published in such publications as *Poetry Northwest*, *Bellingham Review*, *Redivider*, *Mid-American Review*, *Southern Indiana Review*, and *The Collagist*. She is a graduate of the MFA program at Eastern Washington University and the recipient of a grant from the Spokane Arts Fund.

Photo by Ellie Kozlowski